Times Table Time

&

Rhyme

Fabulous Football Times Tables

Christopher Davies

Chris Davies

Copyright © 2019 Christopher Davies

All rights reserved.

ISBN: 9781081486259

Name: _____

Favourite Team: _____

For all the players in the football teams I have coached over the years. I hope you are still enjoying the 'beautiful game'! Teams from Rickmansworth Park JMI, Wigston C of E Primary, Thorpe Hamlet Middle, Mile Cross Middle, Reepham Primary, Wood End Primary, Moat House Primary and Kenilworth Town FC - junior section.

Times Table Time

&

Rhyme

'Fabulous Football Times Tables' is the third title in the successful 'Times Table Time & Rhyme' series, created by Chris Davies.

Chris has worked with primary aged children to develop and test out his latest book of football rhymes, which helps children to learn their times tables in a fun and interactive way.

Chris has over twenty five years experience of teaching primary mathematics and understands how important it is for children to learn their times tables at an early age, for developing confidence and a love of maths.

Thank you

I would like to say a BIG thank you to my editing team (MAC, M and RCD) for their help and feedback in the development of the rhymes and a special thank you to Megan for her creative support with the illustrations and design.

I would also like to say a HUGE thank you to my 'Junior Reading Maths Group' (Finlay, Leen, Mohammed, Josh, Mel and Jake) for their constant feedback and ideas.

Special thanks to authors at Pixabay and Wikimedia Commons for allowing me to use some of their amazing images. (Please see page 37/38 for names and full license details) Many thanks also to the image authors at Dreamtime and Shutterstock.

Thank you to Judy Brook, at Kenilworth Books, for her generous help and advice with sales and marketing.

Finally, I would like to say a massive, BIG thank you to you the reader for buying this book. I hope you enjoy reading the rhymes and that they help you to learn your times tables.

CONTENTS

x1	Who is the Greatest One?	2
x5	England's Euro Dream	4
x2	Pep's Premiership	6
x10	The Catalan King	8
x4	Klopp's Comeback	10
x8	Chelsea's Champion	12
x3	Gunners' Glory	14
x6	Kane at the 'New Lane'	16
x9	Ole Gunnar's Young-Stars	18
x11	White-Hot England	20
x7	Real-Deal Ronaldo	22
x12	Magnificent Moore	24

	Extra Time	26
	Penalty Shoot Out	27
x1	Football for Everyone	28
x9	Fergie Time in '99	30
X2	'Keep me Ups' with Sue	32
	Times Table FA Cup	34
	UEFA Champions League	35

Author's Note:

Most of the rhymes in this book are based on factual events in the football world.

Top Tips for
Fabulous Football Times Table Learners

(Message to children, parents, carers, grandparents and teachers)

1) To achieve the best rhythm for the rhymes, I suggest reading the numbers as follows:

"One 5 is 5 – Three Lions ROAR with pride!"
"Two 5's are 10 – Southgate's MAGIC men!"
"Three 5's are 15 – Can they FIX our nation's dream..?"

This will help create a quicker pace to the rhyme, which will make it read better and help make it easier to learn. ("One times 5 is 5, Two times 5 is 10," will also work well.)

2) You can be read the rhymes on your own, but they will also work very well when reading with a parent, grandparent, sibling or friend. When reading with a partner, sometimes you could read just the numbers and your partner could read the corresponding rhyme.

You read, "One 5 is 5," and they read, "Three Lions ROAR with pride!"
You read, "Two 5's are ten," and they read, "Southgate's MAGIC men!"
You read, "Three 5's are 15," they read, "Can they FIX our nation's dream..?"

This will help you to really focus on the number pattern of the times table. After a while swap over and let your partner read the numbers and you can read the corresponding rhyme. Before long you will know your times tables off by heart!

3) Reading the rhymes in reverse can also be fun and help you learn:

    They read, "Three Lions ROAR with pride!" You read, "One 5 is 5"
    They read "Southgate's MAGIC men!" You read, "Two 5's are 10"

I hope you have hours of fun reading these rhymes and learning your times tables together.

Skill Drills

Fabulous Football Times Table Challenge

Ready to challenge yourself? When you are trying to recall your times table from memory, the rhymes can be used to help you to remember the correct answer. For example, if you are stuck on 7 x 8 = ? Your reading partner can read the corresponding line of the rhyme – "Hazard's flying – fancy flicks!". You will then know that the answer you need rhymes with 'flicks'... That's right, it's 'fifty six' 7 x 8 = 56! Using the rhyme as clues will make learning your times tables more fun and interactive. This will also help speed up your learning.

Times Tables Premier League Penalty Shoot-Out, FA Cup & UEFA Champions League.

Towards the back of the book you will have the chance to put your times table knowledge to the test. First you can use your maths skills in a 'Premier League Penalty Shoot-Out!' Can you beat your opponent and win promotion to the PREM?

For an even bigger challenge you will be asked to answer lots of times table facts in a short time. Can you WIN the 'Times Tables FA Cup' or become a 'UEFA Champions League Times Tables Winner? Good luck!!

x1   Who is the Greatest One?

1 x 1 = 1   Who is the GREATEST one?

2 x 1 = 2   Ronaldo, Messi – WHO?

3 x 1 = 3   Can we PLEASE agree…?

4 x 1 = 4   They both score goals galore..

5 x 1 = 5   Defenders can't survive…

6 x 1 = 6   Their fancy moves and flicks

7 x 1 = 7   Skills that come from heaven

8 x 1 = 8   Thrills and spills they make

9 x 1 = 9   Fab free kicks – so fine!

10 x 1 = 10   Score hat-tricks again and again

11 x 1 = 11   So is it TEN or SEVEN ?

12 x 1 = 12   This question, should we SHELVE?

13 x 1 = 13   TWO of the GREATEST EVER SEEN!

14 x 1 = 14   The Ronaldo Messi GOAL machine!

7 ?   10 ?

10? 7?

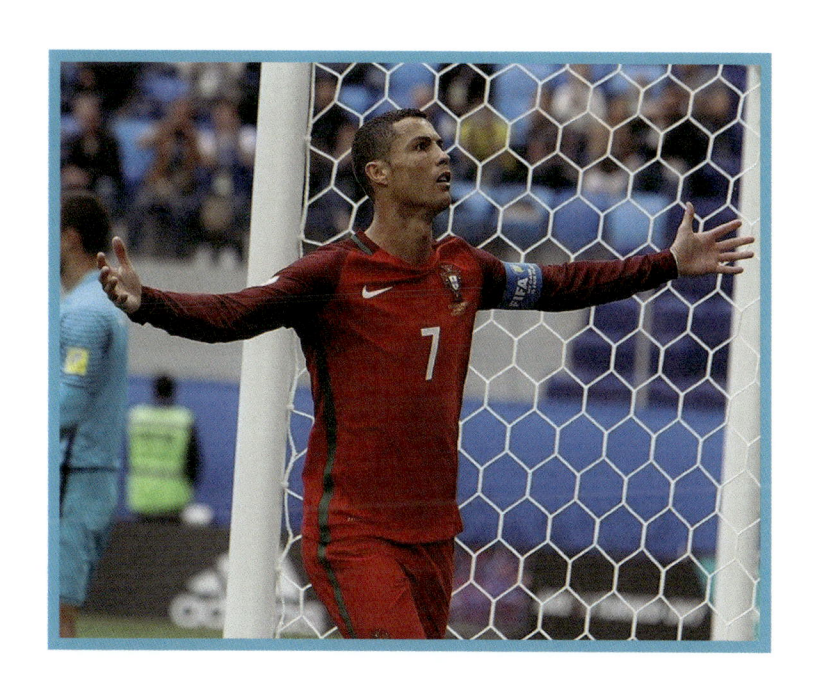

x5   England's Euro Dream

1 x 5 = 5	Three Lions ROAR with pride!
2 x 5 =10	Southgate's MAGIC men!
3 x 5 = 15	Can they FIX our nations dream…?
4 x 5 = 20	In the FINAL – CHEERS aplenty!
5 x 5 = 25	Kane on target - the dream's ALIVE!
6 x 5 = 30	But have we scored too early…?
7 x 5 = 35	A PEN…? NO WAY! That was a DIVE!
8 x 5 = 40	Where's V-A-R? That's NAUGHTY!
9 x 5 = 45	1-1 the score - can we survive…?
10 x 5 = 50	Sterling SUPER - NIFTY!
11 x 5 = 55	A GOAL! We've WON! What a power drive!
12 x 5 = 60	It's COMING HOME – this is HISTORY!!

5

x2 Pep's Premiership

1 x 2 = 2   Come enjoy the view…

2 x 2 = 4   Gasps and goals galore!

3 x 2 = 6   De Bruyne's clever kicks.

4 x 2 = 8   He puts it on a plate…

5 x 2 = 10   Aguero SCORES again!!

6 x 2 = 12   More trophies for the shelves..

7 x 2 = 14   The greatest football ever seen!

8 x 2 = 16   Sterling, Silva – what a team!

9 x 2 = 18   Super City – skills we dream!

10 x 2 = 20   The Etihad's in a FRENZY!

11 x 2 = 22   A Kompany Cracker turns the night SKY BLUE!

12 x 2 = 24   The Premier League is PEP's once more.

Manchester City 1   Leicester City 0
Kompany 70 mins

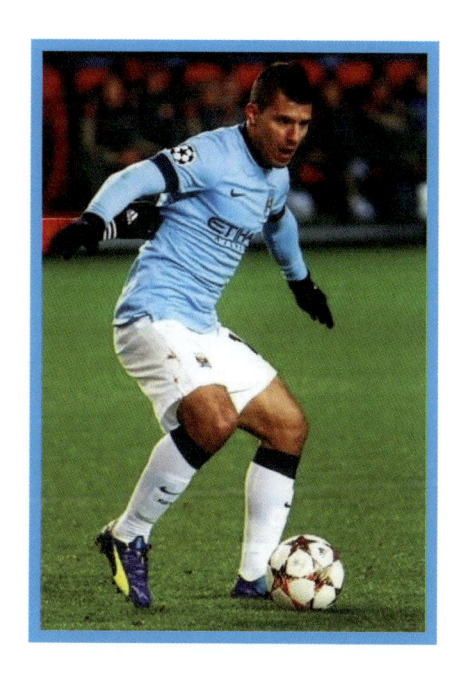

x10   The Catalan King

1 x 10 = 10   A KING amongst mere men.

2 x 10 = 20   Camp Nou in a FRENZY!

3 x 10 = 30   Messi's scored a WORLDY!!

4 x 10 = 40   Another Barca sortie…

5 x 10 = 50   He nets a cheeky chippy!

6 x 10 = 60   Super skills – so twisty

7 x 10 = 70   Defenders spent – on empty!

8 x 10 = 80   Dribbling past so pacey!

9 x 10 = 90   SKILLING players sublimely…

10 x 10 = 100   In the GOAL it THUNDERED!

11 x 10 = 110   Hat-trick-hero - again and again!

12 x 10 = 120   The Catalan King - the BEST for a century!

A prolific goal scorer and playmaker, Messi holds the records for most goals in La Liga (421), most hat-tricks in the UEFA Champions League (8), and most assists in La Liga (164) and the Copa América (13). Messi has scored a total of 575 career goals.

x4   Klopp's Comeback

1 x 4 = 4   A comeback you can't ignore!

2 x 4 = 8   A Houdini-like escape!

3 x 4 = 12   Still pinching ourselves…

4 x 4 = 16   Beating Barca – it's like a dream….

5 x 4 = 20   Klopp's Kop ARE cheering plenty!

6 x 4 = 24   3-0 down - THEN Origi scores!

7 x 4 = 28   But is it just too little too late…?

8 x 4 = 32   Mesmerising Mane dribbling through…

9 x 4 = 36   Two GOALS for Geo – we're in the MIX!

10 x 4 = 40   PENALTIES looming shortly…

11 x 4 = 44   Trent's cheeky corner… A GOAL! UPROAR!

12 x 4 = 48   Miracle night at Anfield, the BEST, am I awake?

Liverpool 4 (4) Barcelona 0 (3)

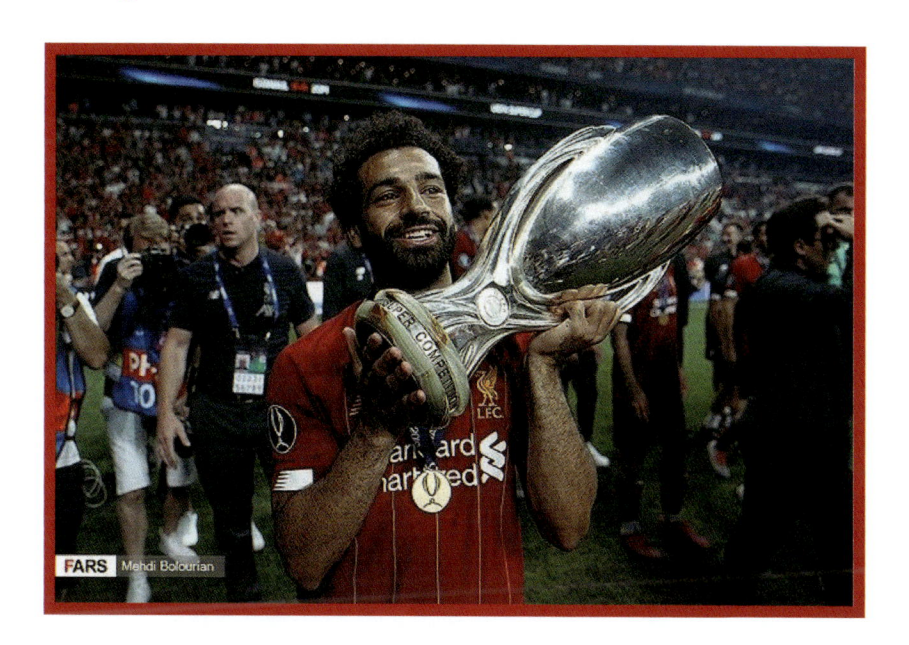

After beating Barcelona in the semi-final, Liverpool went on to beat Tottenham Hotspur 2-0 in the 2019 Champions League Final, Mo Salah and Origi scoring the goals. Liverpool then went on to win the Super Cup against Chelsea on penalties (5-4) with Mane scoring 2 goals.

x8   Chelsea's Champion

1 x 8 = 8   Cheer and celebrate!

2 x 8 = 16   Eden delivers the Europa dream…

3 x 8 = 24   Thrashing the Gunners – GOALS galore!

4 x 8 = 32   A classy header from Giroud!

5 x 8 = 40   Kante super-sporty!

6 x 8 = 48   Pedro pounces – no mistake!

7 x 8 = 56   Hazard's flying – fancy flicks!

8 x 8 = 64   Fans are chanting – "We want more!"

9 x 8 = 72   Goal-hungry Hazard NETS a few!

10 x 8 = 80   A Superstar – no maybe…

11 x 8 = 88   Bows out at the Bridge a Chelsea GREAT!

12 x 8 = 96   Gasps, goals and rolls and his big box of tricks!

Chelsea 4   Arsenal 1

Hazard joined Real Madrid in June 2019 for around £100,000,000.
He made 352 appearances for the Blues and scored 110 goals.

x3   Gunners' Glory

1 x 3 = 3   A RIPPER from Wrighty!!

2 x 3 = 6   Bergkamp's fancy flicks.

3 x 3 = 9   Arsene's GOLDEN time…

4 x 3 = 12   Trophies lined the shelves…

5 x 3 = 15   Skills the Prem had seldom seen.

6 x 3 = 18   Adams, Keown – a defence so MEAN!

7 x 3 = 21   All other teams they just OUT-GUN!

8 x 3 = 24   Now Emery's Arsenal are on the UP for sure…

9 x 3 = 27   Europa FINAL – so close to heaven!

10 x 3 = 30   Battle-scarred but worthy.

11 x 3 = 33   Could AUBA be the new HENRY..?

12 x 3 = 36   Gunning for glory – back in the MIX!

Thierry Henry is Arsenal's record goal scorer with a total of 228 goals.

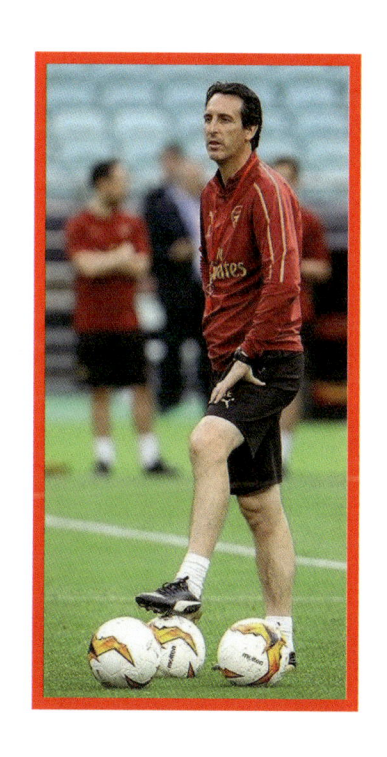

15

x6   Kane at the 'New Lane'

1 x 6 = 6   A trophy drought to fix…

2 x 6 = 12   In the crowd with cousin Kelve.

3 x 6 = 18   A title-test for the goal-machine…

4 x 6 = 24   Kane is class – we all adore!

5 x 6 = 30   Feeling tense and nervy…

6 x 6 = 36   We need more of Moura's magic tricks!

7 x 6 = 42   Son Heung-min is speeding through!

8 x 6 = 48   Ali flicks it to his mate…

9 x 6 = 54   Harry heads home! Hear the New Lane ROAR!

10 x 6 = 60   Please ref – blow up QUICKLY…!

11 x 6 = 66   Poch is running on the pitch…!!

12 x 6 = 72   The PREM at last – our dream came TRUE!!

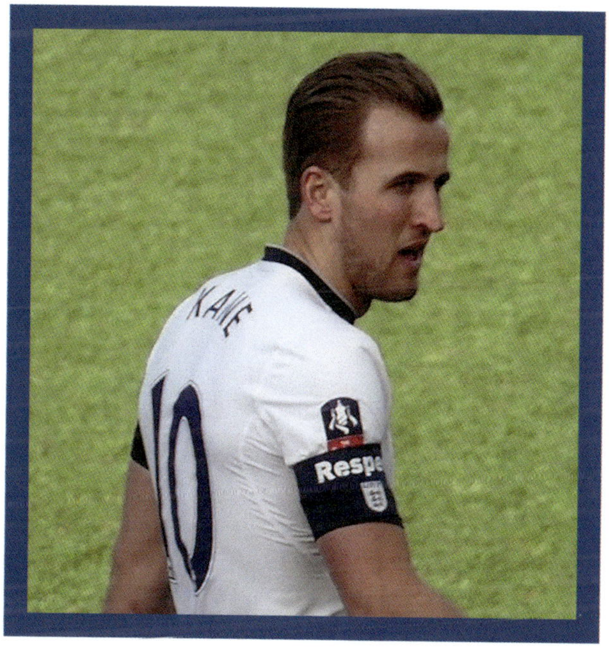
KANE
10

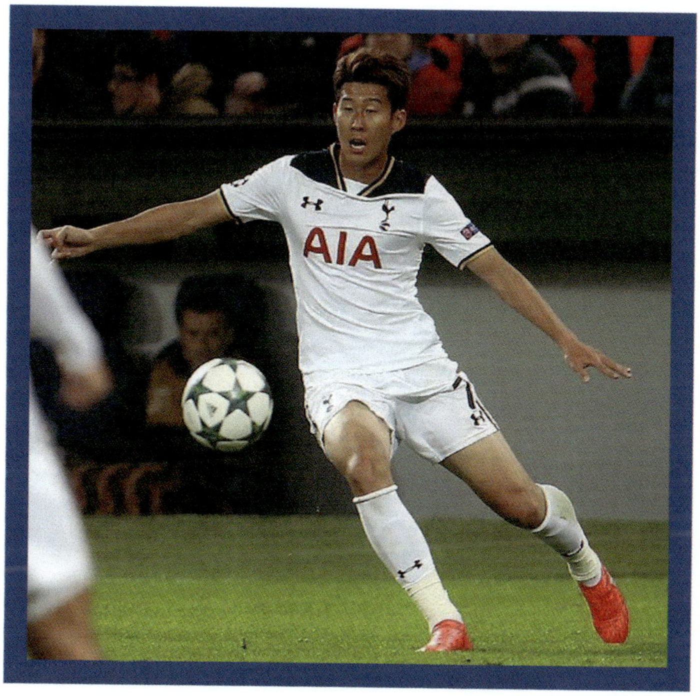
AIA

x9 Ole Gunnar's Young-Stars

1 x 9 = 9   For the 'Fergie Times' we pine…

2 x 9 = 18   When United were the GREATEST team

3 x 9 = 27   Fabulous football made in heaven!

4 x 9 = 36   Now Ole's young-stars are playing for kicks

5 x 9 = 45   Jesse's goal celebration JIVE!

6 x 9 = 54   A Rashford ROCKET! We want MORE!!!

7 x 9 = 63   Martial's skilling and scoring with glee!

8 x 9 = 72   Time Manchester was RED not BLUE!

9 x 9 = 81   Playing with promise – good times to come…

10 x 9 = 90   Pogba curls one in SUBLIMELY!

11 x 9 = 99   James like lightning down the line…

12 x 9 =108   The 'glory days' …? Not long to wait!

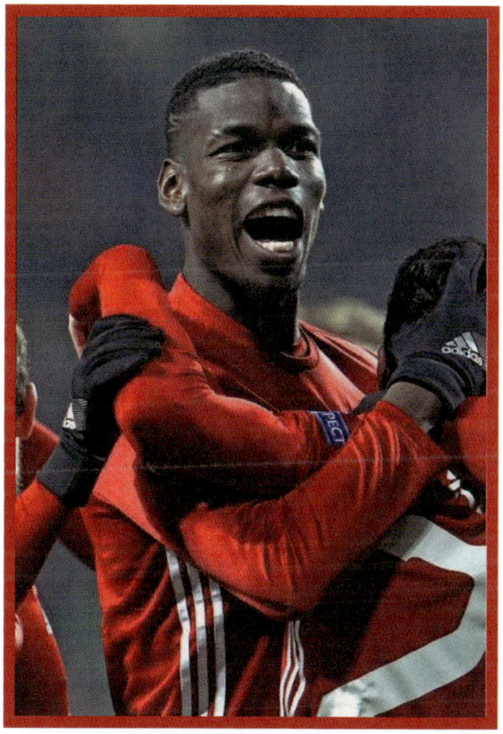

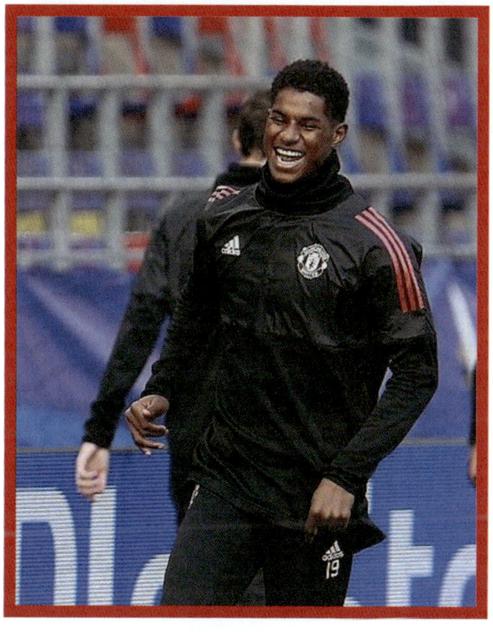

x11 White-Hot Lionesses

1 x 11 = 11   Lionesses close to HEAVEN!

2 x 11 = 22   The World Cup Final - almost through.

3 x 11 = 33   So close... then THAT PENALTY!

4 x 11 = 44   But Neville's lionhearts went out with a ROAR!

5 x 11 = 55   Knocking out nations in their stride...

6 x 11 = 66   Nikita in Paris doing her tricks!

7 x 11 = 77   GOALS! GOALS! GOALS! from White-hot Ellen!

8 x 11 = 88   That Bronze thunderbolt – the net did BREAK!

9 x 11 = 99   Awesome attacking - skills fast and fine...

10 x 11 = 110   Houghton's heroes will fight on again...

11 x 11 = 121   Playing with passion – inspiring the young!

12 x 11 = 132   We will WIN it next time - by a goal or a few!

England striker, Ellen White, was the leading scorer in the 2019 World Cup.

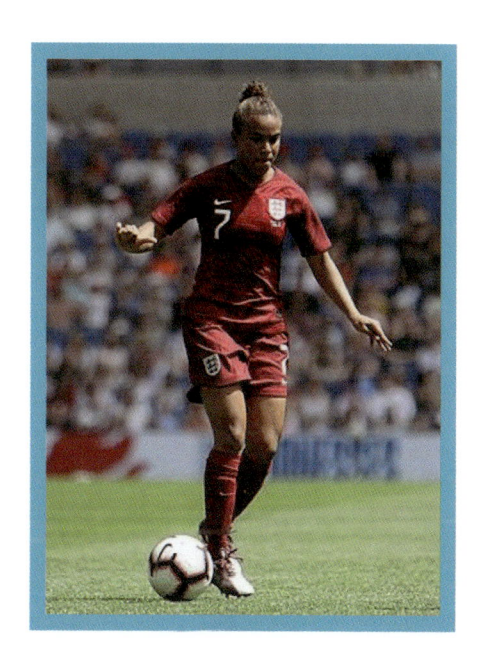

Nikita Parris showing her 'tricky' skills.

x7 Real-Deal Ronaldo

1 x 7 = 7   From Portugal or heaven?!

2 x 7 = 14   The greatest striker the world has seen.

3 x 7 = 21   Hearts and trophies he has won.

4 x 7 = 28   At Madrid he made La Liga QUAKE!

5 x 7 = 35   Real-deal Ronaldo - perfection he strives.

6 x 7 = 42   A winner with Juve and Portugal too!

7 x 7 = 49   Hat-trick heroics - time after time!

8 x 7 = 56   Handsome headers and fabulous free-kicks!

9 x 7 = 63   Pace, power – AGILITY!

10 x 7 = 70   'Goal-Getter' of the century!

11 x 7 = 77   Always first choice in my 'Dream Eleven'.

12 x 7 = 84   RONALDO! RONALDO! You know he will score!

Cristiano Ronaldo reached a career landmark on Monday 14th October 2019, by scoring his 700th career goal in Portugal's Euro 2020 qualifier at Ukraine. Widely regarded as one of the greatest players of all time, Ronaldo holds the record for most goals in the UEFA Champions League (127).

x12 Magnificent Moore

1 x 12 = 12   Into the past we delve…

2 x 12 = 24   The greatest game you ever saw…

3 x 12 = 36   The sixty-six FINAL- all games this 'LICKS'!

4 x 12 = 48   England or Germany - only one could be GREAT…

5 x 12 = 60   Moore on the ball – so NIFTY!

6 x 12 = 72   The scores still level – the tension grew…

7 x 12 = 84   Hurst hits the bar! Was it a SCORE..?

8 x 12 = 96   NO V-A-R … the goal still sticks!!!

9 x 12 = 108   When Hurst nets his third the fans don't wait…

10 x 12 = 120   On they RUN! It's a Wembley FRENZY!

11 x 12 = 132   World Cup Champions! Is it REALLY true??!

12 x 12 = 144   Triumph for England and the great Bobby Moore!

Queen Elizabeth presents the 1966 World Cup to England Captain, Bobby Moore.

England 4   West Germany 2

Bobby Moore leads out the England team at Wembley.

Extra - Time

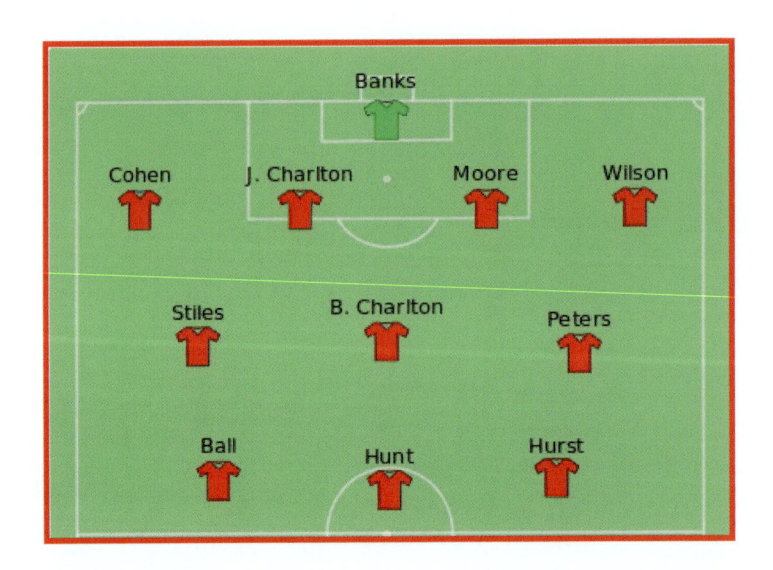

England's 1966 World Cup Final winning team.

Premier League Penalty Shoot-Out

When you think you know a times table really well test it out in a

PENALTY SHOOT-OUT!

Imagine you are at Wembley in the Premier League Play-Off Final and the match has gone to penalties. If you win YOU go to the Premier League!

Rules:

1) You and your partner choose the football teams you want to be and decide which times table you are going to test each other on. e.g. x 7

2) You will have the chance to score the first penalty! Get your partner to ask you a times fact from your chosen times table. For example, it might be 5 x 7 = ?

3) If you get the answer to the times fact correct you score a GOAL!! The score will then be 1 – 0 to you. If you get it wrong, then their keeper saves it and the score will be 0-0. The winner will be the team that scores the most goals.

4) Next it is your partners turn to try and score a penalty. Read them a times fact (from their chosen times table) and if they get it right they score a GOAL, but if they get it wrong, your keeper saves it!

5) After both of your teams have had 5 chances to score a penalty, the penalty shoot-out is over. If you have scored the same number of goals, you can take one more penalty each until someone misses and then there is a WINNER!

Can you become a 'Premier League Penalty Shoot-Out Winner'?

x1 Football for Everyone

1 x 1 = 1	Football for everyone.
2 x 1 = 2	All shirt shades - pink and blue.
3 x 1 = 3	For EVERY ability.
4 x 1 = 4	Beat the keeper – SCORE!
5 x 1 = 5	On the grass we dive…
6 x 1 = 6	A blissful fitness-fix!
7 x 1 = 7	This is our seventh heaven!
8 x 1 = 8	Play every day you wake
9 x 1 = 9	When old or in your prime
10 x 1 = 10	Girls, boys, ladies - men!
11 x 1 = 11	In Derbyshire, Kent and Devon.
12 x 1 = 12	Together or by yourselves..
13 X 1 = 13	The greatest sport there's ever been!
14 X 1 = 14	Respect and fairness – never mean!
15 x 1 = 15	Football for ALL – a winning team!

29

x9   Fergie Time in '99

1 x 9 = 9   It happened in 'Fergie Time'…

2 x 9 = 18   The greatest fight back ever seen!

3 x 9 = 27   'Busby Babes' cheering on from heaven…

4 x 9 = 36   Going out…'til a late United Blitz!

5 x 9 = 45   Teddy on target – the game's still ALIVE!

6 x 9 = 54   Champions League Final, 1-1 the SCORE…

7 x 9 = 63   Red Devils raiding – go Giggsy!

8 x 9 = 72   The Treble's on the line for the Class of '92!

9 x 9 = 81   A classy Ole volley and we've won, won, WON!

10 x 9 = 90   Finishing – oh so TIMELY!

11 x 9 = 99   Fergie's Fledglings stand tall and shine

12 x 9 = 108   That night in the Nou Camp was…

                       …ELECTRIFYING - GREAT!

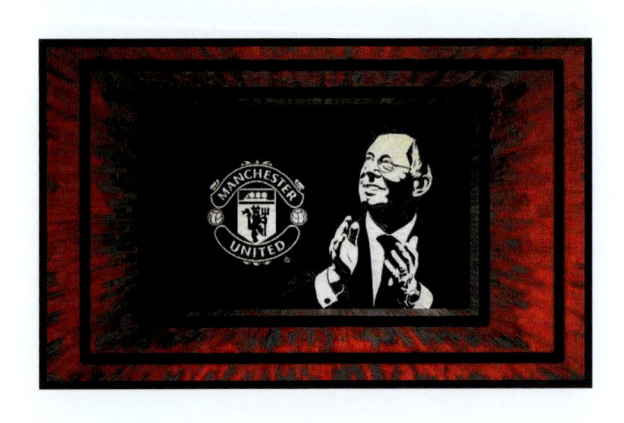

The 1999 Champions League Final

Bayern Munich 1
Mario Basler 10 mins

Manchester United 2
Teddy Sheringham 89 mins
Ole Gunnar Solskjaer 92 mins

The famous Manchester United 1999 'Treble winning' team that won the Premier League, the Champions League and beat Newcastle United in the FA Cup Final 2-0.

x2 'Keep me ups' with Sue

1 x 2 = 2   'Keep me ups' with Sue!

2 x 2 = 4   Can't let it hit the floor…

3 x 2 = 6   Chesties, knees and kicks…

4 x 2 = 8   This is really great!

5 x 2 = 10   Left and right again…

6 x 2 = 12   Better than Uncle Melve!

7 x 2 = 14   Soon we'll make the England team!

8 x 2 = 16   Let's score a ton and make them green!

9 x 2 = 18   Might even get to meet the Queen??!

10 x 2 = 20   Tricks and skills a plenty!

11 x 2 = 22   Sorry Sue I need the LOO!

12 x 2 = 24   "On 99……!!!!!??? - Oh what a BORE!!!!"

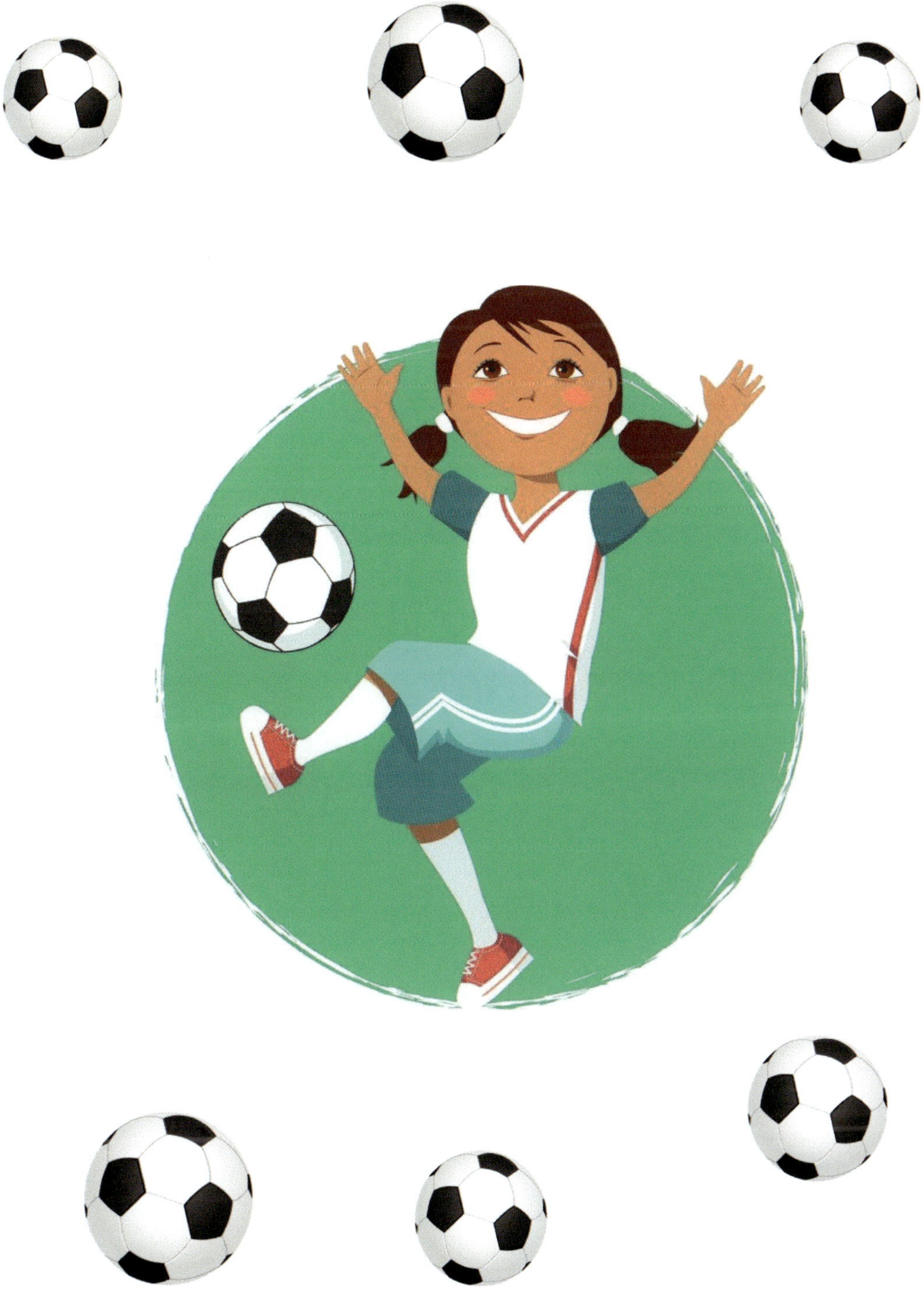

Times Table FA Cup

Are you ready to test your times table knowledge and try and win the FA Cup? If so, photocopy this grid and see how many you can get right in 10 minutes. The first row is the 10 times table – A few answers have been filled in to help you. Can you **score 132 out of 132** and win the **FA Cup**? After each attempt fill in the Date, Time, Score and Target.* (for Target see page 35) **Good luck! You can do it!**

X	1	2	3	4	5	6	7	8	9	10	11	12
10	10	20	30									
5	5	10										
2												
4												
3												
6												
7												
8												
9												
11												
12												

| Date | Score | Time | Target |

UEFA Champions League

Are you ready for an even trickier times table challenge? Can you score 100 out of 100 in less than 6 minutes and become a **'UEFA Champions League Times Table winner'**?

1) Photocopy this grid & put in 10 numbers from 1 – 12 in a **random** order across the top row. E.g. 2,4,5,3,6,9,7,8,12,11. The first number has been put in for you and the answer 10 x 2 = **20**

2) Give yourself 8 minutes to complete as many as you can – no peeping in the book please!

3) Get some help to check your answers and record your score out of 100 and the time and date.

4) To work out your new **Target**, just add on 10. If you scored 45, your new target will be 55. If you score 100 in 8 minutes try and beat your time by 10 seconds and so on. If you score 100 out of 100 in less than 6 mins you will become a **'UEFA Champions League Times Table winner!'**

x	2									
10	20									
5										
2										
4										
3										
6										
7										
9										
8										
12										
Date		Score			Time			Target		

Dear Reader

I hope you enjoyed this book. If you did, please leave me a book review on amazon.co.uk. – I would be very interested in hearing from you. Which rhymes and illustrations did you like the best? Has it helped you to learn your times tables? I hope it has!

How much progress have you made? Have you won the 'FA Challenge Cup' or become a 'UEFA Champions League Times Table Winner'?

If there isn't a rhyme with your favourite football team in this edition, look out for my next book in the series. If you have any ideas, why not try and write your own football times table rhyme?

If you do write one, I would love to see it. Send it to:
cnd26111959@gmail.com

Keep an eye out for my next book in the series which will be out later in 2020!

Best wishes

Christopher Davies

Images used in this book

Special thanks to all the image authors and Wikipedia Creative Commons.

Image & Page	Source	Author
Messi (cover)	Pixabay	Abdullah Munzer
Messi p9	Pixabay	YaNiS2017
Sir Alex Ferguson p30	Pixaby	Nadejda bostanova

Image & Page	Source	Author	Licence
Messi, Ronaldo p3	Soccer.ru	Кирилл Венедиктов	CC Attribution-Share Alike 3.0 Unported
Kane, Lingard group Sterling p5	Soccer.ru	Антон Зайцев	CC Attribution-Share Alike 3.0 Unported
Southgate p5	Soccer.ru	Кирилл Венедиктов	CC Attribution-Share Alike 3.0 Unported
Man city players p7 (slightly cropped)	Own work	Ardfern	CC Attribution-Share Alike 4.0 International
Aguero p7	Soccer.ru	Дмитрий Голубович	CC Attribution-Share Alike 3.0 Unported
Liverpool team bus p11	FLICKR DSC4798	Eric the Fish	CC Attribution 2.0 Generic
Mo Salah p11	Fars News Agency	Mehdi Bolourian	CC Attribution-Share Alike 4.0 International
Hazard, Hazard & Pedro p13	Fars News Agency	Amir Husseini	CC Attribution-Share Alike 4.0 International
Henry p15	FLICKR	wonker	CC Attribution 2.0 Generic
Aubameyang p15	FLICKR	Ronnie Macdonald	CC Attribution 2.0 Generic
Arsene Wenger p15	FLICKR	Ronnie Macdonald	CC Attribution 2.0 Generic

Unai Emery	Fars News Agency	Amir Hosseini	CC Attribution-Share Alike 4.0 International
Kane p17	FLICKR	enviro warrior	CC Attribution 2.0 Generic
Son p17	Soccer.ru	Дмитрий Голубович	CC Attribution-Share Alike 3.0 Unported
Pogba P19 (cropped)	Football.ua	Станислав Ведмидь	CC Attribution-Share Alike 3.0 Unported
Rashford p19 (cropped)	Soccer.ru	Дмитрий Голубович	CC Attribution-Share Alike 3.0 Unported
E. White, N Parris p21	FLICKR	James Boyes	CC Attribution 2.0 Generic
Ronaldo p23	Soccer.ru	Кирилл Венедиктов	CC Attribution-Share Alike 3.0 Unported
Queen & B. Moore p 25	FLICKR Commons mrjohncummings	National Media Museum	Flickr.com/commons
1966 England team p25	Scanned from *El Gráfico*	Unknown	Public Domain
Manchester United 1999 Champions League win.	Winners	Sean Murray (original) Danyele – cropped/RT	CC Attribution-Share Alike 2.0 Unported
Manchester United team for 1999 FA Cup.	Own work	Peejay	CC Attribution-Share Alike 2.0 2.5 3.0 4.0 Int.
England v Germany teams	Die Geschichte der Fußball	ksk-opf	Any purposes.

Image licence links: creativecommons.org/licenses (for full details)   https://flickr.com/commons/usage

Books by Christopher Davies

If you would like to find out about (or purchase) other books written by the author, please visit Kenilworth Books (www.kenilworthbooks.co.uk) or check out the Author's Page for Christopher Davies on amazon.co.uk

Books available include:

Transformer the Tiger Cat

A humorous adventure about a boy who keeps changing things! Connor's peculiar habit gets him into all sorts of trouble, but things get even worse when he makes a birthday wish to turn his pet tabby cat into a tiger… Age 6+

Terrifying Times Tables

Humorous, fun-filled rhymes to help make learning your times tables...

A CHILLING and THRILLING experience!

Themes include being trapped in a Haunted House, Sky-Diving out of a plane and coming face-to-face with Deadly Aliens!

Hours of FRIGHTFUL FUN and LEARNING! 7+

"I bought this for my 8-year-old granddaughter who couldn't put it down. As well as helping to learn her tables it also helped with her reading." Paula

Times Table Time and Rhyme

Catchy amusing rhymes to help make learning your

Times Tables....

EASY & ENJOYABLE!

Popular themes include: snow, football, the seaside, baking a cake, sports day, trips to the zoo & the school disco.

Read aloud with family & friends!

Hours of FUN...

and... LEARNING!   Age 5+

'I use this book with my Year 2 class and they absolutely love it! They are so keen to learn their times tables now. A fantastic book to engage all children and get them learning.'
Ms Nunn (teacher)

Prickly-Pong Island and the Emerald Treasure

TREASURE is a wonderful thing… but is it more important than anything?

Jay finds school difficult but his twin sister Sanjana loves it - so when Dad wins a holiday to a desert island, Jay thinks all his dreams have come true! Maths and spellings tests are happily replaced with climbing palm trees and making friends with the mischievous monkeys.

But living in an island paradise doesn't turn out to be all fun & games and before long, Jay and Sanjana become entangled in a daring real-life escapade they would never have believed possible! Pirates and 'Prickly-Pong' - lost treasure and tattooed tribes. Life soon becomes VERY different from school! Danger is lurking everywhere - something far more terrifying than the most menacing pirate…

A thrilling 'green-themed' adventure set in the islands of the South-Pacific. Full of humour & happiness; sadness & regret; bravery & friendship. 7+

"My 7-year-old son absolutely loved this story… A perfect mix of adventure and suspense. He didn't want it to end and can't wait for the next one in the series." Lucy

In a Spin

It's almost time! The annual St. George's Dance Competition is only days away. Maddy is favourite to win but something serious is bothering her...

Close friend, Jack is a daring Break-Dancer who is going all out to beat his arch rival Justin, but will Jack's fiery temper get the better of him?

All the twists and turns you could wish for in this lively, action-packed, School Dance drama.   Age 8+

"This book is amazing. After reading the first couple of chapters I wanted to read all of it straight away! The character of Maddy is my favourite as she loves dancing like me and I like the end of term dance competition... I loved the ending because it was surprising. I would give it loads more than 5 stars if I could!"   Lottie (Age 9)

Printed in Great
Britain
by Amazon